THE BULL RING REMEMBERED

By the same author:

Birmingham Cinemas
Birmingham Theatres, Concert & Music Halls
Old Ladywood Remembered
Aston Remembered
Tracing Your Family Tree

This book is dedicated to
Dr. Richard Wassell
Professor of Music and
Choir Master at St. Martin's Church
in the 1930's. He was also Conductor
of the City of Birmingham Police Band
period 1923 to 1939. He was a real
gentleman.

THE BULL RING

REMEMBERED

The Heart of Birmingham

and

Market Areas

by

Victor J. Price

with
Foreword by
Maurice W. White, B.A.
Local Historian

BREWIN BOOKS

First published August 1989 by
K.A.F. Brewin Books, Studley, Warwickshire.

Reprinted January 1990
Reprinted February 1992

ISBN 0 947731 59 8

Typeset in Baskerville 11pt.
and made and printed in Great Britain
by Supaprint (Redditch) Limited.

FOREWORD
by Maurice W. White, B.A.

In this Birmingham's Centenary Year of 1989, the "Big Heart of Birmingham, Logo" has emerged as representing the 'Thinking City'. Over recent years the City has done well in depicting its history through numerous excellent Plaques, Murals and Mozaics. One such Mozaic spans the centuries of Medieval growth from the grant of the first Market Charter in 1166, and stands on the site of what used to be the Worcester Street entrance of the Old Market Hall.

The following pages overflow with nostalgia, whether by old photographs, maps, advertisements or personal reminiscences. We all have such memories of the "Real Heart of Birmingham" the BULL RING. Originally as Victor Price states, the Village Green, had but nine families living around it in 1086, and yet, within 80 years, such was its importance, that the Lords de Birmingham had been granted the Royal Charter of Market Rights, this being decades before any other towns in the Midland region.

The Bull Ring first recorded as such in the mid 16th Century takes its name from an Iron Ring, set into the ground just below the row of Butcher's Shops (the Shambles see page 16), to which the Bull would have been tethered and then slaughtered. For many centuries there has been an 'Open Air Market' on this site, and let there be no doubt that the Bull Ring is the 'Pulse of the Brummie' together with St. Martin's, our Parish Church. Multi million pound development must not be allowed to destroy this, our inheritance.

I feel sure that this book will help to keep in the forefront of peoples minds, not only the Bull Ring nostalgia, but also its historical foundation, enabling future generations to understand just what it means to be a Brummie, not only while celebrating the City's first century but in knowing that Birmingham's history, and the Bull Ring in particular, goes back probably 10 centuries.

I recommend this book to every true Brummie.

Maurice W. White, B.A., Local Historian.

Maurice White, is a lecturer in mechanical and manufacturing engineering, primarily in mathematics. For 20 years he has studied the History of Birmingham, and is well known for his Public Lectures on Birmigham life and personalities. Maurice's particular contribution to the Centenary Year was the lecture at the Birmingham and Midland Institute, "10 Centuries of Birmingham Life" which he gave on the 30th. January 1989.

PREFACE

The Bull Ring was, and in my opinion, still is, the Heart of Birmingham. In the Domesday Book, 1086, Bermingham is recorded on the site of the original village green, used for tethering cattle. In 1731 it was known as the Green and, a St. Martin's Church has been on this site since 1263. The Parsonage (or Rectory) was situated at the junction of Smallbrook Street and Pershore Street. The Manor House, residence of the Lord's of Birmingham, was situated 100 yards south of the church, and 40 yards west of Digbeth. The approach to the courtyard was over a bridge which was situated opposite Bradford Street. The house was defended by a moat which originally joined the river Rea at Vaughton's Hole which divided the parishes of Birmingham and Edgbaston at that time. The moat was filled in in 1816, the former stream was diverted from the river Rea to an artificial channel.

This was how the area started and became the heart of our city.

Up to the end of the 18th century the main water supply in Birmingham was available from springs and wells and this, at that time, appeared to satisfy the needs of the population. There was a cock pump, which gave a fine supply of soft water near St. Martin's Church. It was free to the inhabitants and daily there could be seen a succession of people drawing water. Water carts also filled up from this source and from other similar pumps in the area.

During the 19th and 20th century the area had a symbolization of Characters in the area and, one of the earliest remembered was in the 1840's was 'Jimmy the Rock', he carried a tray and sold broken rock. The Barrow Boys, who had to obtain annual licences in order to trade in the area, were issued with numbered arm bands and, in order to be given a pitch in which to trade, their arm bands were removed and placed in a sack by the local police officer. The first one drawn was given a best site, outside Woolworths Store in Spiceal Street, others could select the site required. In the early 1920's 20 Licences were issued and they rose to 25 during the last war years. This was reduced to 18 in 1958.

To name but a few of these characters, Smedley, William (Twiddy), Sparrow (Sprug), Harold Hart, Kennedy, Billy Reeves (Bull Ring Billy), Freddie Jones (Freddie the Fly), Harry Smith (flash Harry), Lou Cohen, (Lou The Jew). Barrow Girl, Emma Brook, she wore a flat cap and an army coat just after the first world war. She used to sell boxes of oranges. Lillian Evans was the black sheep of the Bull Ring, she had a record of 112 convictions for fly pitching and short weight. She was eventually banned from trading in the area. They traded on trestle tables and/or wheelbarrows. At night these were lit by portable naptha hanging lamps, these gave good light and heat to the traders.

The orators corner, was in front of Nelsons Statue. Ernie McCullock was a popular speaker for the downtrodden and under privileged, he was a compassionate man. Percy Shurmer was also popular, he became a Member of Parliament in 1945. Holy Joe, Mr. Waite, was very popular, he arranged collections for poor children and took them to Rhyl, to most their first trip to the seaside, he was a railway worker from Lawley Street Station. Jimmy Jesus, Thomas Hands, gave devoted sermons, he wished to live the life of Jesus. Unfortunately he was killed in a car accident in Earlswood area in 1933. The Salvation Army held services on Saturday nights, they came from Barford Street citadel.

The Bull Ring was alive in those days, the atmosphere was unique, the jostle, the jingle, the excitement, smell of fruit, clothing and cooking. I hope that by reading this book all those memories will come back to you. The area was devastated when it was modernised and lost most of its character. When you hear St. Martin's Church bells ring it does bring back those memories of what it was like yesterday.

Victor J. Price.

"There is land for six ploughs and there are five villeins and four borders; it is worth 20 shillings"

Domesday Book 1086

"The beauty of Birmingham, a good market town in the extreme parts of Warwickshire, is the street going up along almost from the left side of brooke, up a meane hill. There be many smithes in the towne that use to make bites, and a great many naylors. Soe that a great part of the towne is manitained by smithes, who had their iron and sea-cole out of Staffordshire"

Leland 1538

Probably in no other age or country was there ever such an astonishing display of human ingenuity as may be found in Birmingham..

Robert Southey. (1744-1843 poet, essayist and historian)

CONTENTS

1

SAINT MARTIN'S CHURCH

THE PARISH CHURCH OF BIRMINGHAM

The earliest mention of this church was in 1263. In 1873, under the direction of J.A. Chatwin, the whole building, with the exception of the tower and spire, was carefully demolished and rebuilt in the style of the previous churches. It was re-opened on the 12th July 1875.

The Reredos, at the base of the East Window, was described by Sir John Betjeman as the finest in the Midlands. The centre is a representation of the Last Supper and the other four panels show the entry into Jerusalem, the cleansing of the Temple, and the Agony in Gethsemane and the Kiss of Betrayal. The Tombs near the chancel are effigies of Sir Fulk de Bermingham (c.1350) and Sir William de Bermingham, the latter being the oldest monument in the city. The Choir stalls were carved out of the roof timbers of the mediaeval church. Above them in the roof is the 'reserve' choir, twenty stone minstrels with a variety of instruments.

The Chantry Chapel was the Clodsdale Family Chapel until 1547, dedicated to the Blessed Virgin Mary. The window was restored in 1958, and recalls this dedication.

The Guild Chapel is also now known as the Thorne Memorial Chapel. It was restored by the Thorne family in 1956 in memory of their son James Thorne, an American who was killed in action over Arnhem in 1944. The organ, which was originally built in 1906 was moved to this chapel at that time.

On the 10th April 1941 the church, and other parts of the Bull Ring were very badly damaged in an enemy air raid. The main damage was around the main entrance to the church in Spiceal Street. All the windows were blown out, debris was everywhere. First Aid Repairs were completed on the 14th September 1941.

If you would like a few minutes, prayer, peace and contentment, visit the church, for it is open daily from 9.30 am to 4.30 pm.

The Altar and East Window at the Parish Church

The Pulpit in front of the Chancel

The Altar in 1989.

The Guild Chapel, this is also known as the Thorne Memorial Chapel

Marriage of Harry Broughton to Amelia Cook at
St. Martin's Church, Bull Ring, on the 30th September 1939.

Watch Night Service, held in the Markets Air Raid Shelter on the 31st December 1941, conducted by Canon T.Guy Rogers, M.C., B.D., The Rector of Birmingham.

BIRMINGHAM PARISH CHURCH
St. Martin's, Bull Ring.

UNVEILING OF THE
Birmingham City Battalions
Memorial

14th, 15th and 16th BATTALIONS
THE ROYAL WARWICKSHIRE REGIMENT

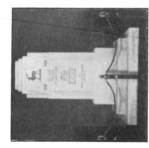

Sunday, 12th November, 1933
3.30 p.m.

Order of Service

Organist: RICHARD WASSELL.
MUSIC:
"Lieder ohne worte," No. 27..............*Mendelssohn*
Andante Sonata in G, Opus 1-4..............*Beethoven*
Finale "Pathetique" Symphony..............*Tschaikowski*

The Unveiling

THE RECTOR,
THE LORD MAYOR,
CAPT. D. NEAL (14th Battalion),
LIEUT.-COL. COLIN HARDING, C.M.G., D.S.O. (15th Battalion),
LIEUT.-COL. GRAHAME DEAKIN, D.S.O. (16th Battalion)

will proceed to the Memorial accompanied by

GENERAL SIR R. B. STEPHENS, K.C.B., C.M.G., who will unveil the Memorial with these words:

"I unveil this Memorial in honour and ever grateful remembrance of the officers and men of the 14th, 15th and 16th Battalions of the Royal Warwickshire Regiment, who gave their lives for their country in the Great War, 1914-1918."

"See ye to it that these shall not have died in vain."

The Last Post.

TWO MINUTES SILENCE.

DEDICATION by
CANON T. GUY ROGERS, M.C., B.D., Rector of Birmingham; Chaplain to the King.

"In Faith and Love and in the Christian hope of immortality I dedicate this Memorial to the memory of our comrades of the 14th, 15th and 16th Battalions of the Royal Warwickshire Regiment, who died for us in the Great War."

Reveille.

ANTHEM (*Stainer*).

What are these that are arrayed in white robes, and whence came they? These are they which came out of great tribulation, and have washed their robes and made them white in the blood of the Lamb.

Therefore are they before the throne of God and worship day and night in His temple. They shall hunger no more, neither thirst any more; neither shall the sun light on them, nor any heat. For the Lamb which is in the midst of the throne shall feed them and lead them unto living fountains of water, and God shall wipe away all tears from their eyes.

2

RECTORS OF THE PARISH CHURCH OF BIRMINGHAM

1294	Baldwin de Insuld
1300	Thomas de Hinklegh
1304	Stephen de Segrave
1304	John de Ayleston
1336	John Irynge
?	Robert de Shuteford
1349	Walter de Sedgeley
1354	James de Dumbleton
1369	Hugo de Wolvesley
1396	Thomas Darnall
1412	William Thomas
1414	Richard Slowther
1428	John Hill
1428	John Waryn
1432	William Hyde
1433	John Armstrong
1433	John Wardell
1436	Henry Symon
	Thomas Lynes
1474	Humphrey Jurdan
1474	William Moore
1504	Richard Sutton
1529	Richard Dudley
1536	Richard Myddlemore
1554	William Wraxham
1578	Lucas Smith
1640	Samuel Wills
1643	(. . . . . Roberts (Minister)
	. . . . . Whitehead (Minister)
	. . . . . Slater (Preacher)
1661	Samuel Wills
1661	John Riland

1672	Henry Grove
1693	William Daggett
1723	Thomas Green
1728	Thomas Tyrer
1732	Richard Dovey
1771	William Chase
1772	John Parsons
1779	William Hinton
1781	Charles Curtis
1829	Thomas Moseley
1846	Dr. John C. Millar
1866	William Wilkinson
1897	A.J. Robinson
1901	J.W. Diggle
1905	I. Denton Thompson
1910	J. W. Willinck
1919	Edward Grose-Hodge
1923	T. Guy Rogers
1948	Bryan Stuart Westmacott Green
1970	Albert Peter Hall
December 1984 - January 1986 Interregnum	
1986	John Graham Wesson

The author when he was a choir boy in the church
period 1930-35.

8

3

SOME LANDMARKS IN THE HISTORY OF THE BELLS AND
RINGERS OF ST. MARTIN'S BIRMINGHAM

c.1705   St. Martin's bells are made a ring of eight, the first in the area. The art of change-ringing was still in its infancy.

1755   The first "peal" (5,000 changes or more) rung by the "St. Martin's Youths", as the ringers were then known. Very few bands of ringers had acquired the necessary technique for such a performance at this date.

1772   A ring of 12 bells created at St. Martin's - one of only seven such rings in existence at the time.

Before the end of the 18th Century, the St. Martin's Youths had rung several notable peals in and around Birmingham.

1814   St. Martin's ringers won a silver cup for the best ringing at the opening of the new bells at St. Nicholas, Liverpool.

1846   The first performance of "Thurstans' Four-Part", a very famous composition which solved a mathematical puzzle that composers of peals had wrestled with for many years.

1867   A visitor to Birmingham commented: "The St. Martin's ringers are masterly performers, and I left the belfry highly delighted.... (It was) one of the most perfect performances of the sort I ever heard."

1901   A record-length peal (11,111 changes) rung at St. Martin's in 8 hours 2 minutes, the longest in a series of record peals which had taken place at intervals since the 1780s.

1924   The first ever broadcast of change-ringing was from St. Martin's, live on a Sunday evening. Many compliments were received by the ringers from across the country.

1950   A.P. Smith, a noted and long-standing ringer at St. Martin's, became Lord Mayor of Birmingham.

1976   The annual national competiton for fine ringing on 12 bells was

	established, and since then the St. Martin's team has won on eight occasions, an unrivalled record.
1983	The 500th peal of St. Martin's. No other belfry has such a continuous and prolific tradition over so long a period. This peal ("Orion Surprise Maximus") is the most complex piece of change-ringing on 12 bells ever achieved by a local band of ringers.
1985	The national ringing contest at Canterbury Cathedral won by the St. Martin's team. We received television coverage.
1986	By invitation of the St. Paul's Cathedral ringers, London, H.M. Queen Elizabeth's 60th Birthday peal there was conducted by a member of the St. Martin's Band of Ringers.
1988	Bell-founders' and architects' reports having been obtained because of increasing concern about the condition of St. Martin's bells (last restored 1928), plans are going forward to create the world's first ring of 16 bells.
1989	A new peal of 16 bells, to replace the old 12 bells was made possible in May of this year, as a gift, from the Witton based international company, IMI. A great gift for the Centenary year.

BIRMINGHAM STAGE-COACH,

In Two *Days* and a half; begins *May* the 24th, 1731.

SETS out from the *Swan-Inn* in *Birmingham*, every *Monday* at fix a Clock in the Morning, through *Warwick*, *Banbury* and *Alesbury*, to the *Red Lion Inn* in *Alderfgate ftreet*, *London*, every *Wednefday* Morning: And returns from the faid *Red Lion Inn* every *Thurfday* Morning at five a Clock the fame Way to the *Swan-Inn* in *Birmingham* every *Saturday*, at 21 Shillings each Paffenger, and 18 Shillings from *Warwick*, who has liberty to carry 14 Pounds in Weight, and all above to *pay One Penny a Pound.*

Perform'd (if God permit)

By Nicholas Rothwell.

The Weekly Waggon fets out every *Tuefday from the Nagg's-Head in Birmingham, to the Red Lion Inn aforefaid, every Saturday; and returns from the faid Inn every Monday, to the Nagg's-Head in Birmingham every Thurfday.*

Note. *By the faid Nicholas Rothwell at Warwick, all Perfons may be furnifhed with a By-Coach. Chariot. Chaife, or Hearfe, with a Mourning Oach and able Horfes, to any Part of Great Britain, at reafonable Rates: And alfo Saddle Horfes to be had.*

This coach proceeded to London down the Bull Ring. The Swan Inn was at the top of the Bull Ring, 148, New Street. Swan Passage, at the top of the Bull Ring led direct to the court-yard of the Inn. It was later called the Swan Hotel. The Rotunda is now on this site.

Public Offices, Magistrates Court and Prison, Moor Street.

Prior to 1800, Birmingham was run by Street Commissioners and the main centre of administration was in the Bull Ring and High Street but, they had no official place of meeting. In 1807, these Public Offices were erected and opened, the first meeting took place in December of this year. The ground floor was used by the Street Commissioners, the upper floor as the Magistrates Court, the rear of the premises was the Prison. The High Bailiff at this time was Henry Perkins, the Low Bailiff, Thomas Small and the constables were Joseph Blunt and Thomas Whateley.

12

A Survey of the area was made in 1750 by Samuel Bradford, of the houses and inhabitants in the area, details as follows:-

AREA	HOUSES	INHABITANTS
Edgbaston Street	151	879
Moor Street	195	1076
Moat Lane	43	252
Park Street	156	944
Spiceal Street	41	249
Bell Street	39	179
Phillip Street	38	213
Corn Cheaping	29	162
Digbeth	303	1646
	995	5600

In later years all these houses were demolished and the inhabitants moved to other areas of the city. Business premises were then erected.

(See map on page 15 for locations)

SELLING OF WIVES IN ENGLAND

In 1773, three men and three women went to the Bell Inn in Edgbaston Street, Birmingham and made the following singular entry in the toll-book which is kept there:-

"August 31.1773, Samuel Whitehouse of the parish of Willenhall, in the county of Stafford, this day sold his wife Mary Whitehouse, in open market, to Thomas Griffiths, of Birmingham, value one shilling. To take her with faults (signed) Samuel and Mary Whitehouse. Voucher, Tho. Buckley of Birmingham".

The parties were all exceedingly well pleased, and the money was paid down, as well for the toll as purchase.

from The Antiquary's Note-Book. July 1887. Vol. 16.

William Hutton the first Birmingham Historian 1723-1815.

He came to this Town when he was 17 years of age, from Derby and his first impression was as follows:-

"The buildings in the exterior of Birmingham rose in style and elegance. Thatch, so plentiful in other towns, was not to be met with in this place. I was much surprised at the place, but more so at the people. They were species I had never beheld. I had been among dreamers, but now, I saw men awake, their very step along the street shewed alacrity. I had been taught to consider the whole 24 hours as appropriated for sleep but I found a people satisfied with only half that number".

After endeavouring to find work and being unsuccessful he perceived two men in aprons eyeing him with some intention. They approached near, "You seem", says one, "by your melancholy situation and dusty shoes, a forlorn traveller, without money and without a friend". He assured them he was. "If you choose to accept a pint, it is at your service. I know what it is myself to be distressed". He replied that he would receive any favours with thankfulness. They then took him to the Bell Inn in Philip Street and gave him a drink and bread and cheese. They also procured a lodging in the neighbourhood where he slept for 3 half pence."

This meeting took place as William Hutton was sitting in the vicinity of the Market Cross in the Bull Ring area.

This extract was written on Tuesday 14th July 1741.

MARKET CROSS.

14

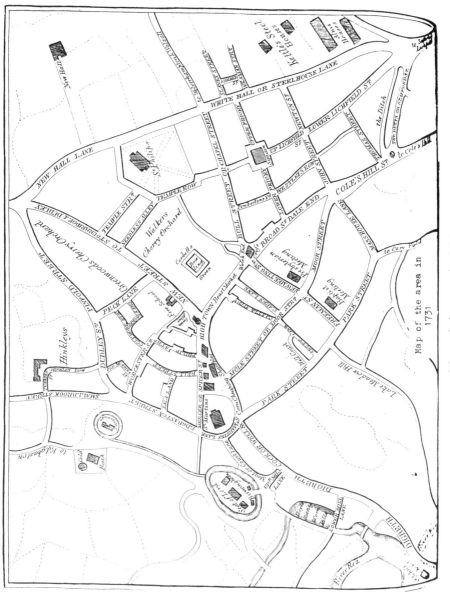

Map of the area in 1731.

15

The Bull Ring in the 18th Century, the building in the foreground
is The Market Cross, this was demolished in 1784. The buildings
in the centre were known as "The Shambles", a row of butchers
shops immediately down the centre of the area.

A stage coach operating in the Bull Ring (see advertisement page 11).

Taken in 1883.

The Bull Ring on a market morning.

17

THE BULL RING, BIRMINGHAM.

Late 19th Century.

At the beginning of the
20th Century.

18

Early 1900's.

Taken from the Parish Church
in the 1950's, note the bomb
damage area on the right of
the picture.

Ladies selling lavender
in the area, period 1901.

A Kerb Merchant selling wire working toys, outside the Market Hall
and on the corner of Bell Street.   This photograph was taken in
April 1895.

Pony and trap, coming out of Bell Street. In the background is the Fish Market. Leading off this street, towards Worcester Street end, was an opening named, 'The Poultry' in this area William Grimsley had stables for 100 horses. There were also several poultry houses erected on stilts, the eggs provided were sold in the market. There was also the Midland Stores, licensed premises, run by Miss Florrie Page, this was very popular with the fish traders and customers. Period 1909-1920's.

This guide, published in 1914 gives you full details of how to reach the Bull ring from all districts in Birmingham.

The Bull Ring in the 1930's.

The Bull Ring, taken from St. Martin's Church Late 1920's.

Junction of High Street, Moor Street and Bull Ring. This photograph was taken on the 29th July 1952. John Baskerville, born in Wolverley, Worcs. in 1706, became a very well known printer. In 1737 he resided at No.22, Moor Street and his interests then were in a lucrative branch of japanning. In 1745 he took over land in Easy Hill, now known as Easy Row, this covered 8 acres and 2 furlongs. He had a building erected on this site, next to the Hall of Memory in Cambridge Street. The modern building now on this site is called, Baskerville House.

1945 showing the bomb damage.

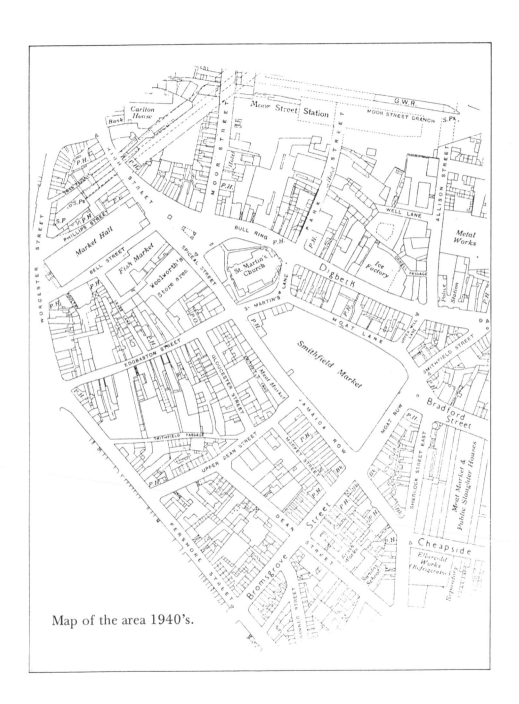

Map of the area 1940's.

C. GREEN & Son. 10 Bull Ring. (Opened by Cornelius Green in 1895 closed 1934). The gentleman on the right is Walter Herbert Green, the other gentleman is one of his assistants, Fred Tullett, this shop opened in the late 19th century and was there for many years. They specialised in all type of leather goods, boxing gloves, footballs, purses, cases for travelling etc., all were made on the premises. One year Mr. Green made a 6ft high leather football and the Police borrowed this for their Sports Day in Aston Park, police on horse back played football with it.

At the rear of the premises was a court yard, known as Golden Court it had 4 cottages and a lodging house called Pump Lodgings, this was run by a Mr. Davis. He used to take in tramps and charged them 2p per night. In those days they were gentlemen and could be trusted. In the centre of the court yard was a water pump, one of many erected in the area for the supply of water. In his younger days, Sir Adrian Cedric Boult, the well known musician, rented a room in the court yard to practice, he was the founder of the BBC Symphony Orchestra 1930 to 1950. He was born in 1889 and died in 1983.

One interesting aspect of these premises is, that, under the premises, leading off the cellar was a tunnel leading to St. Martin's Church. It is not known why this tunnel was originally built but, it could have been an escape route from the original churches,

1944 prior to demolition.

In the 1930's numbers 11 - 12 were occupied by the Birmingham Midland Motor Omnibus Co.Ltd., and the Midland Red Parcels Express Office. Across the road outside the entrance to St. Martin's Church was the Midland Red bus terminus, they came up Digbeth into the Bull Ring and left by going down Spiceal Street. A very popular terminus and very active. They had a Sports and Social Club at 123, Digbeth.

These are typical Bull Ring scenes in the 1930's and 40's.

Taken from the
Market Hall area.

Bull Ring Scenes.

Bull Ring Scenes.

4

NOSTALGIC MEMORIES

Nostalgic memories come flooding back.
When I think about the heart of old 'Brum'.
The sights, and sounds, and those characters around.
That always made the Bull Ring, so much fun.
For, there was something for all, in that Bull Ring.
From bargains to Con-men with their tricks.
Holy Joe, and Jimmy Jesus preached religion.
Percy Shurmer and his mates, preached politics.

Remember the old gal, by the Market Hall steps?
With her back to the hand rail barrier.
Like a record that's stuck, she would keep crying out.
    "Git yer 'andy carrier".
By Nelsons statue, the escapologist performed.
He was the Bull Rings own Houdini.
In Mexican Sombreros, on Piano Accordian.
Played Dave Dodd, and Tony Mancini.

Their Music was really delightful.
The crowd were soon tapping their feet.
As those two went through their repertroire
    on the corner of Phillip Street.
For music the Bull Ring was noted.
With its Central Salvation Army Band.
And those lasses with their tambourines.
They put on a show very grand.

There were day old chicks, on sale up there.
And of course the corn cap man.
And on a cold and frosty morn,
To the Baked tater cart we ran.
If you sprinked all this, with fish market aroma.
And a peel of St. Martins bells.
Added the "Sweet Violet" calls, of the flower girls,
And the Barrow Boys, loud raucous yells.

30

You would have some idea, of what I'm describing.
Within this little Rhyme.
But, how can you portray the Bull ring?
It was a place, that was created by time.
The Luffwaffe tried to destroy it.
When it paid some nightly calls.
But it only took the roof off the Market Hall.
It could not destroy the walls.

It was the planners, in their wisdom.
That tore the old Bull Ring apart.
In order to create a concrete jungle.
A city without a heart.
Our heritage has gone now for ever.
To its memory, I always will cling.
I shall see all the ghosts of those characters.
Whenever St. Martin's Bells ring.

Bill Waters.

This photograph was taken on the 10th June 1962.

Going down from the Fish Market on the corner of Bell Street
to Edgbaston Street and Jamaica Row. 1950's.

William Timpson Ltd., Boot and Shoe Dealers was at 17a, Spiceal
Street, two doors from Woolworths and next door to Smarts the butchers.
Miss Joan Davies worked there as a cashier, period 1936-37. She worked
from 9.00 am - 7.00 pm Monday to Thursday, 9.00 am - 8.00 pm on
Friday and 9.00 am - 9.00 pm on a Saturday. On this day she was also
expected to serve customers . The work was very hard, the manager was
a real slave driver. Her wages were 12/6 per week. Today, school leavers
are being offered by Super Markets over £100.00 per week.

In 1924 when the Spread Eagle public house was at 14, Spiceal
Street, at the rear was Spread Eagle Yard which housed members of the
florist business, Mrs. R.H. White, Mrs. Emily Pritchard, Walter Butler,
Mrs. Catherine Chipman, Mrs. May Wilson, Mrs. Emma Parkes, Mrs. Emily
Roger, Merrick and Joseph Caffery.

Going up from the Market Hall entrance, do you remember Chapmans Bird Shop on the corner of Swan Passage? Proprietress Miss Ada Mary Chapman.

NELSON'S STATUE

This was erected in the Bull Ring and officially opened on the 25th October 1809 in memory of Lord Nelson 1758-1805, British Admiral and naval hero killed in the battle of Trafalgar. It was made of bronze and designed by Sir Richard Westmacott. It had a pedestal, palisades and a gas lamp on each corner and it cost £2,500, this was raised by voluntary subscription. It is inscribed:-

'This statue, in honour of Admiral Lord Nelson, was erected by the inhabitants of Birmingham A.D. MDCCCIX'.

These two photographs depict, top a memorial day service, attended by the Lord Mayor of Birmingham, Councillor J.R. Balmer, on the 25th October 1954. The bottom one was taken in 1897 showing floral tributes in his memory.

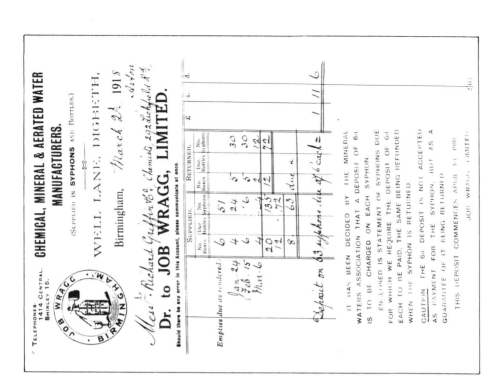

Telephones.
1414 Central.
Shirley 16.

JOB WRAGG — BIRMINGHAM

CHEMICAL, MINERAL & AERATED WATER MANUFACTURERS.

(Supplied in SYPHONS and BOTTLES.)

WELL LANE, DIGBETH,

Birmingham, March 2ⁿᵈ 1918

Mess. Richard Griffin & Co, Chemists 292 Lichfield Rd, Aston

Dr. to JOB WRAGG, LIMITED.

Should there be any error in this Account, please communicate at once.

	SUPPLIED.			RETURNED.		£	s.	d.
	No. Boxes	No. Bottles	No. Syphons	No. Boxes	No. Bottles	No. Syphons		
Empties due as rendered:								
Jan. 24	6	51				30		
Feb. 15	4	24	5		5	30		
Mar 6	6	6	5		5	12		
	4		12		12	72		
	20	/35	12	12	due n			
	/2	.72	72					
	8	63 due n						

Deposit on 63 syphons due @ 6d each = 1 11 6

IT HAS BEEN DECIDED BY THE MINERAL WATERS ASSOCIATION THAT A DEPOSIT OF 6d IS TO BE CHARGED ON EACH SYPHON. ENCLOSED IS STATEMENT OF SYPHONS DUE FOR WHICH WE REQUIRE THE DEPOSIT OF 6d EACH TO BE PAID, THE SAME BEING REFUNDED WHEN THE SYPHON IS RETURNED.

CAUTION. THE 6d DEPOSIT IS NOT ACCEPTED AS PAYMENT FOR THE SYPHON, BUT AS A GUARANTEE OF IT BEING RETURNED.

THIS DEPOSIT COMMENCES APRIL 1st 1918.

JOB WRAGG, LIMITED.

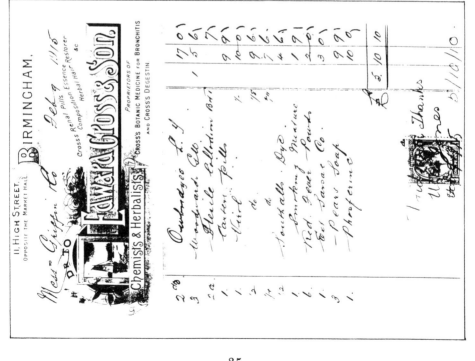

11, HIGH STREET, BIRMINGHAM.
Opposite the Market Hall

Feb 9 1918

Mess. Griffin & Co

Dr. to Edward Cross & Son

Chemists & Herbalists

PROPRIETORS OF Cross Renal Pills Essence Restorer & Composition Herbal Hair Restorer &c

CROSS'S BOTANIC MEDICINE FOR BRONCHITIS AND CROSS'S DEGESTIN

		£	s	d
Outridges L 4			17	0
Woodward Co	1		5	6
Alcolic Pollution Bot			7	
Tartan Pills			9	9
Steel do	½		10	0
do			9	9
do			7	
Southalls Dye			4	6
Compy Mixture		1	9	
Red Beaut Pounds			2	0
Feet Savat Co			3	0
Pears Soap			9	9
Phosferine			10	0
		£ 5	10	10

With Thanks
5/10/10

DINING ROOMS IN THE AREA

Charlie Miles stalls in the old market hall was a very popular establishment, he occupied stalls 83 to 90.   You could have a lamb dinner for 10d, two vegetables and beef for 11d.   He opened daily at 12 noon.

Mrs. Margaret Mountford, at 9 & 10, Phillips Street was very popular. She used to stand in the window carving the joint of meat expertly.   She was always dressed immaculately.

REDFERN's run by George Amos, at the bottom of Jamaica Row at No. 3, Bromsgrove Street in the 1930's, this was later taken over by Frederick Thomas Preece.   You could get a pork dinner for 1/-, 2 faggots and mushy peas and mashed potatoes for only 9d.

Barton's, 12 Moat Lane.   William Henry Miles at 6, 7 & 8 Bell Street. Alfred George Treadwell, 55 Jamaica Row.   A.A. Daniels, 17 Jamaica Row.   T. Hall, 50 Moor Street.   Antoni Lupi, 149 Moor Street.   Alice Trigg, 94 Digbeth.   C. Hollings, 62 Edgbaston Street.   Mrs. Florence Smallwood, 40 Upper Dean Street.

The aroma from these, and other establishments, was fantastic, really made your mouth water.

You could also get a lovely snack from Woolworth's Cafeteria.

1906

This establishment was demolished when Woolworth's first store was erected in 1922.

5

SATURDAY NIGHT UP THE BULL RING

I'm looking through the windows of time, to the Bull Ring on a
     Saturday night.
Can you see me there?   I'm with our dad, what a lovely sight.
Are you with me now, take a closer look, do you remember the
     things you see?
You can walk with me and our dad up the Bull Ring for a cup of tea.
There's the carrier-bag lady — I liked her, she was ever so nice.
And there's the flower-seller, what lovely flowers — you'll get some
     at a good price.
The barrer boys are shouting loud, sometimes they frighten me.
Dad's just popped in to the fish market — to get some kippers
     for our tea.
We'll stop and watch the strong man in all his chains.
He's here every Saturday, even if it rains.
Dad's bought me some penny wilks, and I've got some of them
     sweet fishes.
We had em from the rag alley, you know, where they sell second
     hand dishes.
Dad's bought mom some troach drops, I think our shopping's done.
Saturday night at the Bull Ring's over, but didn't we have fun!
The curtains have closed on the windows of time, and I'm not a
     child anymore.
The days of the Bull Ring on a Saturday night are just a memory,
But we can look back through the windows of time, we can look
     back and see.
Just how good it was, and what we got from it then, and what we
     feel as we think of it now,
I'll never forget it as it was — I won't I know, that's a vow.
I don't want to forget those happy times — I don't do you?
We've had a look through the windows of time, and that's the
     best we can do.

Patricia Hambridge.

37

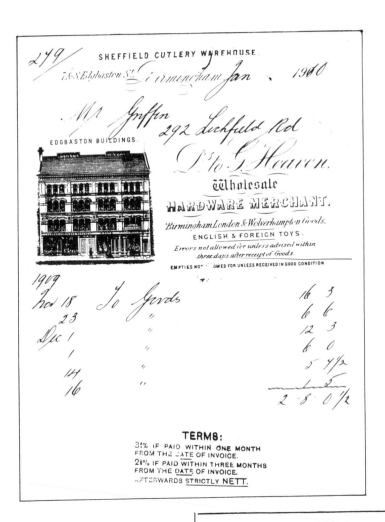

279/
SHEFFIELD CUTLERY WAREHOUSE.
T. & S. Edgbaston St. Birmingham Jan . 1910

Mr Griffin
292 Lichfield Rd
D^r to G. Heaven.
Wholesale
HARDWARE MERCHANT.
Birmingham, London & Wolverhampton Goods.
ENGLISH & FOREIGN TOYS.
Errors not allowed for unless advised within three days after receipt of Goods.
EMPTIES NOT ALLOWED FOR UNLESS RECEIVED IN GOOD CONDITION

EDGBASTON BUILDINGS.

1909
Nov 18   To Goods   16   3
   23   ,,   6   6
Dec 1   ,,   12   3
   1   ,,   6   0
   14   ,,   5 7/2
   16   ,,
                              2 · 8 · 0 1/2

TERMS:
3½% IF PAID WITHIN ONE MONTH FROM THE DATE OF INVOICE.
2½% IF PAID WITHIN THREE MONTHS FROM THE DATE OF INVOICE.
AFTERWARDS STRICTLY NETT.

These were the popular names of cigarettes and tobacco in the 1930's.
'Black Cat' was another popular brand and Will's Woodbines, these cost
2d for a small packet of 5. They could all be obtained from
Hawkesfords the Tobacco Traders at 4 Spiceal Street.

Afrikander

—that's all

BUT THAT'S EVERYTHING!
That one word means the joy of
pipe-hood to me. And I've got
a few years' smoking experience
to look back at !

*"It saves and
satisfies"*

7½ ᴰ PER OZ

MIXTURE or FLAKE

Issued by Cohen Weenen & Co. Ltd.

ARMY CLUB

The best cigarette
ever sold at 10 for 6d

CIGARS.

Extraordinary Value in Cigars,

SMALLMAN & CO.,

MOOR STREET (near the Bull Ring).

All Cigar Buyers should call and see our brands
and prices. Established 1876.

March 1907

Smooth to the lips
are the 'Ivory' tips

When you come
to the end of a
perfect day —

DE RESZKE

De Reszke Virginias 10 for 6d.
'Ivory'-tipped or Plain

—of course!

Court of Back to Back Houses in Digbeth,
early 19th century.

TRIPE HOUSE, DIGBETH.

1906

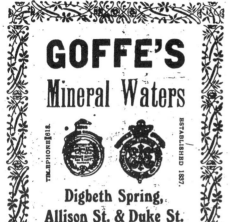
1880's to 1920's.

1879

1914

41

POLICE STATION, DIGBETH, BIRMINGHAM

This building was erected to the design, and under the supervision of the Birmingham City Engineer and Surveyor, and occupies a prominent position at the corner of Digbeth and Allison Street. The frontage to Digbeth is faced with Portland Stone, and that to Allison Street with Ruabon facing bricks, having Portland Stone dressings. The building was erected by T. Elvins & Sons, Birmingham. The foundation stone was laid by Mr. Councillor A.D. Brooks, Chairman of the Watch Committee on the 29th May 1911. It was then under the authority of the Birmingham City Police, 'A' Division and in the 1939/44 war period Divisional Orders were issued by Chief Superintendent Beamon Harrison.

Christmas Meat Show, 1890.

D. HEDGES & SON

"THE ROYAL PURVEYORS."

6, SPICEAL STREET, BIRMINGHAM,

Exhibit the following Choice Specimens in their Great Meat Show—

1.—**Three Pens** of grand Pigs, bred and fed by **Her Majesty the Queen**, at the Prince Consort's Show Farm, Windsor.

2.—**Two Pens** of grand Pigs, bred and fed by **His Royal Highness the Prince of Wales**, at Sandringham, specially for D. Hedges and Son.

3.—**One Pen** of choice Pigs, bred and fed by **His Royal Highness the Duke of Connaught**, at Bagshot Park.

4.—**200 Choice English Pigs.**

5.—**100 Choice Welsh Pigs.**

6.—**100 Choice Irish Pigs.**

This Great Meat Show will be continued with fresh supplies till Christmas Eve.

TONS OF THE FAMOUS ROYAL CAMBRIDGE SAUSAGES & MELTON PIES.

Messrs. D. HEDGES AND SON have as usual been honored with extensive orders from Her Majesty the Queen and His Royal Highness the Prince of Wales.

DOUGLAS. DOUGLAS. DOUGLAS.

For Clean Newspapers, Paper Bags of every description. Plain White Paper, Crease Proof Brown Paper, Cap and Tissues, Twines, Stationery, Day Books, Shop Books, and Ledgers. Tin and Card Board Tickets in stock and written to order.

NOTE THE ADDRESS:

DOUGLAS, 11, Jamaica Row,

Opposite Old Meat Market, BIRMINGHAM.

1909

J. & F. FLETCHER,

WATCH AND CLOCK

MANUFACTURERS,

4, JAMAICA ROW,

BULL RING.

N.B.—WATCHES, CLOCKS, AND MUSICAL BOXES REPAIRED ON THE SHORTEST NOTICE—*Workmanship Guaranteed.*

1879

Telegrams—"MEAT, BIRMINGHAM."

Established over 60 years.   Telephone No. 153.

A. A. SHORTHOUSE,

WHOLESALE AND RETAIL

High Class Meat Purveyor,

Hotel and Restaurant Contractor.

Special Quotations to Schools, Clubs and Large Consumers.

Jamaica Row, BIRMINGHAM.

Wholesale Depot—CITY MEAT MARKET, BRADFORD ST.

Deliveries to the Suburbs daily.

1906

6

THE OLD BULL RING AND MARKETS OF BIRMINGHAM,

MEMORIES AND REFLECTION BY NEVILLE CRATHORNE.

My memories and connections with the Old Bull Ring area are from my childhood days right through to the days when the new Bull Ring shopping centre was built, and now even that is all to be changed.

As a schoolboy, I attended Greenmore College in Carrs Lane and later in Union Street and many happy hours were spent during the lunchtimes watching and listening to the host of traders, speakers, entertainers and the constant chatter of the stall holders. There was also the Market Hall with its magnificent clock and the stalls selling fish, vegetables, flowers and the one aisle where dogs, cats, rabbits, birds etc., gave a great interest to all. There was a large open type restaurant where the chef cut roast beef from what seems to be a whole cow. In addition the fish stalls selling shrimps, cockles, oysters and those so delicious jellied eels.

The centre of the Bull Ring, near Nelsons Memorial, gathered all the buskers. A man who apparently swallowed petrol and then blew it out of his mouth in a fine spray which he would light rapidly turning it into a great flame. I remember when he said, "I will blow a flame right up to the weather cock on the top of the church, and, if you don't believe me you can climb to B. . . and I'll singe your wiskers". The finish was that he explained he had to keep a clear throat, as a choke or cough could make him swallow the flame, so he then sold his cough lozenges. Others were bound up with chains from which they escaped, like Houdini. Some did card tricks and others thumped tables and steps as they expounded fiercely their religious and political views, rather like a miniature Hyde Park Corner. Never a dull moment with the fruit and flower sellers on the roadside and the two men who sold "Alkazar Blades" (Razor Blades) and "Billys Weekly Liar" (rather like an early edition of Private Eye).

During the war, Godfrey Baseley (of Archers fame) used to provide information on the weeks events, speaking from a pair of steps just outside Oswald Bailey, Army and Navy Stores, acting for the Ministry of Information. Saturday afternoon and evening the whole roadway was taken up by crowds milling round, no traffic could even consider getting through and the shops round the side of the roadway; were able to sell off their unsold produce, this was in the days before fridges were readily available and great bargains could be obtained by anyone willing to wait till late evening for a special offer of chickens, turkeys etc.

Many of the shops in the Bull Ring will be remembered by those older citizens from the pre-war days. Oswald Baileys, the Army and Navy Store on the corner of Moor Street, I well remember buying a telescope (it was really an ex army or navy gunsight), for a few shillings, a wonderful bargain and they also had an excellent range of clothing, boots and similar items.

The grocers by the market hall, where butter was cut off a huge slab and deftly made into small packets by the salesman using a pair of wooden paddles. Also bacon, which was cut off at any thickness desired by the customer. At the top of High Street was an auction room where watches, jewellery, sheets, blankets, etc., were sold at low prices and on the opposite side was Burtons The Tailors, managed by a Mr. Smith. There before the war I purchased my first evening dress tails, at under £5.00 and that suit lasted me for years, it only had to be changed because of my change in size and remember, as an entertainer I had to give it constant wear. Woolworths opposite the Church, then was still a 3d and 6d store, with further up the road, Peacocks and a 'Penny Bazaar'. An excellent Radio Shop, where I well remember buying radio kits to make up early shortwave sets. Lower down, into Digbeth below the Church, an uncle of mine had a Barbers Shop, Branfords and even further down was Tabberners where the finest White Pudding I have ever tasted used to be sold.

The Bull Ring owed a lot of its popularity, of course, to the fact that it was the main entrance to Birmingham for people coming in from London and the south, as the Coventry Road, Stratford Road, Alcester Road and other main roadways converged, with in addition the Moor Street Railway Station, with passenger and goods terminals, so during the whole of the day there was a general flow of people arriving and going in that area. In the early morning passenger trains from Stratford on Avon line, (known as the North Warwickshire Line), rolled into Moor Street Station every few minutes, bringing in hordes of workers to the City, and, even earlier the Goods Yard received piles of goods for the Market Dealers. Never, however, in my early years did I imagine that I should have such a connection with the Bull Ring area as I eventually did, during the war years. Not being in the forces, due to a low medical grade and being in a reserved occupation, I applied for 'membership' of A.R.P. (Air Raid Precautions) and was allocated the District One Control Centre in Digbeth. The building was the old Fyffes Banana Offices and, as no doubt readers will remember, not much traffic of Bananas into this country during the war! The Centre was a combination of the three services, A.R.P., Police and Fire, a mixture too of full time workers and volunteers, a number of the latter like

45

myself, became full time 'residents', spending every night at the centre. We all became a very friendly and happy team, under the direction of our Senior Officer, Norman Garfield Tomey, with his three sub officers Bert Marshall, Victor Ambler and Howard Long.

N.F.S. Officers included Cliff Stackhouse, Walter Wellum and Police Officers Sgt. Biggs and Sgt. Laurie Rutter. A goodly number of ladies served in the telephone room, both full time and volunteers, names which come to my mind include Mrs. Hadley, Mrs. Rutter (Laurie's wife), Mrs. Billy Robinson, Mrs. Baird (who had two daughters there as well, Rosa and Marjorie), Gwenda Lorraine Hitch etc. etc. The male volunteers who, as I have mentioned before, like myself lived-in were Harold Cave, Jack Bland, Buster Mason, whose wife also was a volunteer telephonist. I do know, sad to say, that most of these names are now no longer with us, but we became a very close friendly team and I am sure actually enjoyed our curious part in the war.

Naturally, we visited the local hostelrys, in particular the Royal George on the corner of Park Street. The publican, Bob and Gladys Burrows, had a parrot named Maurvita, there was a curious story about her. Bob came to notice that, when an air raid was over Birmingham, or even aircraft passing over, en route to Manchester, Liverpool etc., Maurvita, who normally was a terribly noisy bird, went silent from the afternoon onwards. We all decided that, as in those days the enemy aircraft were directed on their course of evil intent by means of a radio beam, that Maurvita could in some strange way pick up the sound on the radio signal, like dogs can hear whistles that the human ear cannot, and she came to realise that when she heard that sound she was in for a lot of other noises, bangs, bumps etc. Another very funny feature of Maurvita was that the publican had previously had a small very 'yappy' dog, and Maurvita would imitate the dog's bark in a remarkable manner.

Many of the market men of those days used to come into the pub, including Ted the Railways Rat Catcher, he often had with him a small ferret which was in his coat pocket and it shook the odd stranger, to see a small furry head pop out of his coat pocket. Others there included Bill Saunders, well known for his Crab stall in the old Market. All a most convivial crowd.

The great Church of St. Martin's situated at the entrance to the Bull Ring, dominated the scene as well it should, being the Parish Church of Birmingham. Further up, in the centre, was the Nelson Memorial, seen by so many but not too many people knew exactly what it was to commemorate, as no doubt they passed it at great speed heading for the public toilets below!

Adjacent to the Bull Ring, Moor Street led up to the Railway Station of the same name, on the left hand side was a well known cafe, the Express Cafe. The owner, Tony, an Italian, had to leave it during the war and it was looked after by Peter Durrando the well known marathon runner, who years back earned fame by falling down and being helped to

46

the tapes by over zealous spectators, which had the result of losing him the winning title, however, Queen Alexander was so moved that she presented him with a medal herself, which was regarded by Peter as more valuable than the actual trophy.

The Bull Ring played a great part in my life and I was both delighted and honoured to offer my contribution to this book. It will be a book that will interest and intrigue old Birmingham citizens wherever they may be and should also provide a reflection of the past to todays people too.

7

MARKETS IN THE AREA

The open-air markets have been in this country, at least since Roman Times, Britain's most durable trading institution. Birmingham was given A Charter of Marketing Rights in 1166 when Henry II, granted this to Peter de Bermingham. Birmingham has been a marketing town now for over 800 years.

A change in the control of the Marketing Rights took place in 1807, when the Town Governors, or, as they were then called, "The Commissioners of the Birmingham Street Act", contracted for the market tolls. In 1824 the Commissioners purchased outright from the then Lord of the Manor, Mr. Chrisopher Musgrave, the marketing rights and tolls for the sum of £12,500, and these they controlled until 1851, when, by the Birmingham Improvement Act, the marketing rights and all the powers appertaining to them, together with the rights of the borough, were transferred to the Town Council, in whom they are now vested. The markets have been greatly extended and improved from time to time.

Smithfield Market was built on this site. It was constructed at a cost of £2,449, plus the cost of the land and premises which came to £3,223.00. It was opened on Whitsun Fair Thursday, 29th May 1817. The cattle market was previously held in Dale End, the pig market in New Street, the Hay and Straw market in Ann Street, (now known as Colmore Row). All these markets were transferred to this new market when it opened. The Hay Market was held on Tuesdays, and the Beast Market on Thursdays. At the West side of the market was a weighing machine and office, for the purpose of weighing hay and cattle etc. There was a common pound and the Keeper's House adjacent to the Market place. The site was adjacent to Jamaica Row, Moat Row and Moat Lane.

SMITHFIELD MARKET, Moat Lane entrance. A very busy area. The original Rag Market was held here. It opened at 1.00 pm. on Tuesday and Saturday. The main gate was closed just prior to the opening and a large crowd would be waiting for it to open. The bell went at 1.00 pm and the porter shouted, "Wait for it", and everyone rushed in. It was a very popular and busy market area. At No. 20 was Glover & Burley, at 18 James Baragwanath & Co.Ltd., and at 22-23 Francis Nicholls Ltd., just a few of the Fruit Salesmen in the area. Period 1930's.

MARKET HALL, Bull Ring entrance, situated between Bell Street, and Phillip Street, the other entrance was in Worcester Street at the top of Queens Drive. The foundation stone was laid on the 23rd February 1833, the architect was Charles Edge. It was completed and officially opened on 12th February 1835, the total cost being £73,266, of which £44,800 was the cost of acquiring the site and properties thereon.

It was illuminated by gas lighting. A number of Rules and Orders were approved, no person was allowed to smoke tobacco in the Hall under a penalty of 5/- for each offence. No person was allowed to keep any dog in the Hall, nor were visitors allowed to bring their dogs inside. No person occupying any stall was allowed to wash or clean vegetables in the Hall after 9 o'clock in the morning. The rent charges was a penny per square foot per day, and there was an additional charge for every basket, not containing more than one bushel, of 1½d a day.

In 1851, a handsome bronze fountain, surrounded by figures representing various manufactures of flowers, fish and fruit, designed and erected by Messenger and Sons. This was placed in the middle of the Hall. This later proved an obstruction to trade and some forty years later was removed to Highgate Park.

The Hall covered a site of 9,600 square yards and was 365 feet long and 106 feet wide and had four walkways. It accommodated 600 stalls. The Market Clock was erected in 1936 and destroyed during an air raid on 25th, 26th August 1940, the entire building was burnt out leaving only the wall standing, these were demolished in 1962 when the area was redeveloped. The Manzoni Gardens now cover this site.

Market Hall, Worcester Street entrance.

Only the Big Bell of this clock survived the bomb damage.
Does anyone know what subsequently happened to it?

51

The interior of the MARKET HALL, the gentleman in the centre of the gangway was the Town Crier, Jacob Wilson. The original fountain is in the background. Period 1890.

The CITY MARKET AND ABATTOIR, Bradford Street, opened in 1895. It was built on the site of the Circus Baptist Church. It had 20 adjacent slaughtering booths and the site covered 3½ acres. In 1965, the abattoir was modernised to comply with new legislation on hygiene and cruelty to animals, this resulted in three modern slaughter lines, one capable of cattle throughput of 60 beasts per hour, one for sheep and calves at 300 per hour and the third for pigs. These improvements were considered to be among the fastest and most efficient in the country.

The Wholesale Fish Market situated in Bell Street and on the corner of Spiceal Street was opened in 1869 and enlarged in the 1880s. J. Vickerstaff & Co.Ltd., were one of the Wholesale Fish Traders in this market. The firm was originally opened in 1827. These photographs show the interior of a section of this market. It was all demolished in 1958 when the inner ring road was being constructed.

Birmingham
Corporation Markets

SMITHFIELD WHOLESALE FRUIT AND
VEGETABLE MARKET.

CITY MEAT MARKET AND ABATTOIRS.

WHOLESALE FISH MARKET.

MONTAGUE STREET CATTLE AND PIG
MARKET.

MARKET HALL.

ST. MARTIN'S RETAIL MEAT MARKET.

BULL RING OPEN MARKET.

GOSTA GREEN OPEN MARKET.

Total Area of the Markets : approximately 9 acres.
Population served : over 2,000,000, covering a
radius of 40 miles.

*Deal with the Birmingham Markets, one of the
largest and best distributing centres in the country.*

MARKET OFFICES,   H. W. WATERS,
MOAT LANE,   *Superintendent of the Markets.*
BIRMINGHAM, 1.

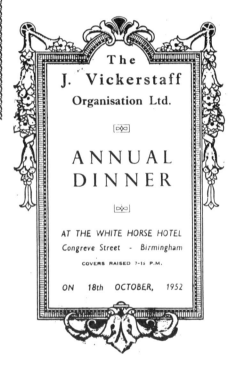

The Birmingham
Wholesale Fish Salesmen's

OUTING.

✝

Motor Tour to
Birdlip and Broadway.

Wednesday, June 5th, 1929.

Tickets 15/-

The
J. Vickerstaff
Organisation Ltd.

⬖

ANNUAL
DINNER

⬖

AT THE WHITE HORSE HOTEL
Congreve Street - Birmingham

COVERS RAISED 7-15 P.M.

ON   18th   OCTOBER,   1952

This map indicates the area that will be covered by the massive new Wholesale Market Complex, this was compiled by Tom MacNeece in 1974. The site covers 21 acres. The shaded Rows and Streets will be covered by this complex.

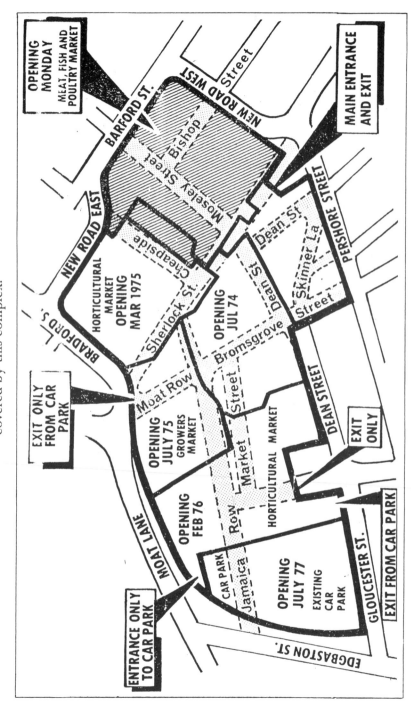

The new WHOLESALE MARKETS PRECINCTS, area Pershore Street and Barford Street. In February 1974 phase 1 of the scheme, the new Fish, Meat and Poultry Markets, were opened.   On the 13th of October 1976 the new Horticultural Market was officially opened by H.R.H. Princess Anne, in the presence of the Lord Mayor, Councillor Harold Powell, the Lady Mayoress and Councillor E.W. Shepherd, the Chairman of the Markets Committee.   The site covered 21 acres.   This photograph shows H.R.H. walking down one of the walkways, from left to right are depicted Bill Patrick - groundsman, Tom Platt, Neville Finnemore, Stan Griffiths, Mrs. H. Brooks, Mr. C.T. Brooks, H.R.H. and Gordon Baragwanath.

8

PUBLIC HOUSES

These played an important part in the lives of residents, business people and visitors to the area, they were social venues for get-togethers for concerts, sing songs and various shows.   There were over 25 in the area and the majority of these no longer exist.   The following details and photographs will, I hope, bring back those happy memories of yesterday.

The licensees indicate by No.1 were managers in 1924, No. 2 in 1944.

GRAND TURQ
34 Bell Street corner of
    Lease Lane   1. T.F. Fletcher.   2. T.P. Collier
BLACK SWAN HOTEL
5 Bromsgrove Street   1. Mrs. E.B. Evans   2. N.F. McCoy
AUSTRALIAN BAR
48 Bromsgrove Street   1. Not there then.   2. Jn. Rickerby
NEW INN HOTEL
191-192 Bromsgrove Street   1. H.L. Jeacock.   2. A. Cemm
CASTLE & FALCON
109 Digbeth   1. A. Russell.   2. W.J.T. Wiley
WAGON & HORSES
14 Edgbaston Street   1. R. Barlow.   2. Closed down
THE COMET
5 High Street   1. W.E. Nelson.   2. Closed down
LION & LAMB
17 High Street   1. W. Brown.   2. Closed down
BROOK'S VAULTS
51 Jamaica Row   1. F. Holliday.   2. F. Brown
  (It was originally known as The Criterion)
PLOUGH & HARROW
81 Jamaica Row   1. S.R. Fisher.   2. F.W. Doran
WOOLPACK HOTEL
8-9 Moor Street   1. F.W. Butler.   2. J. Blower

SWAN HOTEL
148 New Street   1. Mrs. A. Butler. 2. Closed down
PHOENIX HOTEL
3 Park Street   1. P.Vincent-Bennett. 2. E. Freeman
 (It was originally known as Old Phoenix Inn)
THE BOARD INN
7 Phillips Street   1. Mrs. L. Lord.   2. A. Garnett
SPREAD EAGLE
14 Spiceal Street   1. Samuel Rich.   2. Closed down

STEVENS BAR, 149 New Street and 89 High Street, top of the Bull Ring area.   Closed for trading after permitted hours on the 25th March 1958, upon expiration of lease.   Manager, 1. R.E. East. 2. W.S. Allport.   An M & B House.

59

SMITHFIELD ARMS, 47 Jamaica Row.
Manager 1, George Ameghino. 2. Mrs. D.E.
Caldicott.   An Ansells House.

CROSS KEYS, 91 Jamaica Row, corner of Sherlock Street.
Manager 1. G.J. Bunn. 2. J.W. Jesson.   An Ansells House.

ST. MARTIN'S HOTEL, corner of St. Martin's Lane
and Jamaica Row. 1.C.H. Mitchell. 2. E.C. Cox.
An M & B Hotel, very popular. It closed in 1944.

BOARD VAULTS, 56 Worcester Street, corner of Bell
Street. Manager 1. F.R. Andrews. 2. A. Summerfield.
An Ansells House.

BIRMINGHAM ARMS, 1 Moat Row.   Next door at 577 was S. Beeny
& Co. Outfitters.   Sherlock Street East is on the left of the picture,
which was taken on the 1st September 1957.   Manager 1. L.A. Chantrill.
2. Mrs. Emily Stokes.   An M & B House.

A HOME FROM HOME.

"The Market"
TEMPERANCE HOTEL,
19 & 21, MOAT ROW,
(Opposite the Markets) **BIRMINGHAM.**

Good Commercial Room. Personal attention given
by the Proprietors E A. & M. A. FRANCIS,

Sparkbrook, Small Heath and Moseley Trams
pass the door.

Tea, Bed and Breakfast, from 3/6

January 1909

The TALBOT, 24 Moat Lane.   Manager 1.
Ted Lippey. 2. T.W. Gibson.   An Ansells House.

The BELL INN, 7 Phillips Street. Manager 1. Mrs. L. Lord.
2. A. Garnett. It closed for trading after permitted hours
on the 27th January 1958. Peacocks Store side entrance
was next door, the main entrance being at 97-98 High Street.
An M & B House.

The SYDENHAM HOTEL, 43 Edgbaston Street on the corner
of Pershore Street. It was originally called The Criterion P.H.
Manager 1. H. Alexander. 2. J.L. Thornhill. An Atkinsons House.

TAMWORTH ARMS, 5 Moor
Street. Closed for trading on the
6th November 1955. Manager 1.
J.H. Jephcott. 2. D.R. Farr. An
M & B House.

WHITE HORSE, 51 Moor Street
Manager 1. H.T. Patrick. 2. F.C.
Griffiths. An Ansells House.

THE HOP POLE, 43 Pershore Street, corner of Upper Dean Street.
Manager 1. F.J. Freeman. 2. W.H. Young. An Ansells House.

The **ROYAL GEORGE**, 143 Digbeth. This photograph was taken on the 26th July 1951. The one below shows how the new R.G. looks like, this photograph was taken on the 25th September 1964. Manager 1. H. Beaumont. 2. R.W. Burrows. An M & B House.

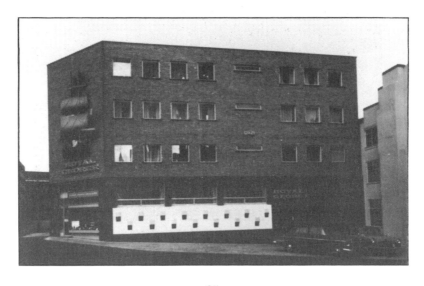

OLD PUMP TAVERN, 8½ Bull Ring. This was situated at the back of No.8. Licencee in 1890 was G.W. Ballard, it closed a few years later.

The **DROVER'S ARMS**, 346 Bradford Street, on the corner of Smithfield Street in the vicinity of the Meat Market. This photograph was taken in 1901. Manager 1. A.F. Green. 2. Mrs. A. Green.

9

ENTERTAINMENT

MOOR STREET THEATRE, Moor Street.
    Opened in 1740 and is the earliest recording of a theatre in Birmingham. It was not a purpose built theatre. The opening performance being an Oratorio with Vocal and Instrumental Musick. In August 1744 The Tempest was presented. (see small advertisement for full details). On another occasion an Evening of Entertainment was arranged, 'For the benefit of Dr. Heighington and Mr. Gunn'. Several musical compositions were performed. Owing to the cold weather, at the time, the theatre was warmed by fires kept burning for two days before the performance. After the concert a Ball was held for members of the public purchasing pit tickets. Although attendance at the theatre was, when it opened, satisfactory, it eventually closed in 1764 and the building was taken over by the Methodists and converted into a Chapel. John Wesley, one of the founders of the Methodists, preached there at the opening service.

MOOR ST. THEATRE
August 1744
By a Company of Comedians from London
The present evening being the 29th of this
instant will be revived
THE TEMPEST
(or *The Enchanted Island*)
as altered by Mr. Dryden and
Sir William Davenant concluding with a
Grand Masque of
NEPTUNE and AMPHITRITE
No person can be admitted back stage on account
of the machinery
Boxes and Stage: 2/6   Pit 2/-   Balconies 2/-
To begin punctually at 7 o'clock
VIVAT REX

A PLAYBILL OF 1835

New Minor Theatre,
ALLISON-STREET, DIGBETH,
FOR THE BENEFIT OF

Mr. ROGERS,
LATE OF THE THEATRE ROYAL

On Monday, June 29th, 1835.

The Evening's Entertainments to Commence with the Favourite Play of the

STRANGER
OR, MISANTROPHY & REPENTANCE.

The Stranger .... Mr. COOKE. (of the Theatre Royal.)
Baron Steinfort . Mr. SINCLAIR. | Count Winterson.. Mr. T. DAVENPORT.
Solomon. Mr. J. C. SMITH, (of the Theatre Royal.) | Francis...Mr. ROGERS, (of the Theatre Royal.)
Peter. Mr. BROWN. | Tobias . Mr. HALLEN. | Stranger's Children. . Miss and Mast. COOKE
Mrs. Haller .... Mrs. A. COOKE. (Of the Theatre Royal, for this Night only.)
Countess Winterson...... I. . Mrs. COOKE.
Charlotte . Miss ADELAIDE COOKE. (All of the Theatre Royal.)

SONG by Mr Hallen,—THE NERVOUS FAMILY.

The whole to conclude with the laughable Farce of the

ACTRESS
OF ALL WORK!!!

Buskin (a Country Manager) Mr. HALLEN. | Frederick (his son)......Mr. F. HARRISON.
Marie, (an actress of provincial celebrity) Miss ADELAIDE COOKE.
Bridget (a country gawky) .... Miss ADELAIDE COOKE!
Flourish, (a first rate London actress, Bridget's) ..... Miss ADELAIDE COOKE!!
Goody Stubbins, (a deaf, amorous old lady at eighty, Bridget's grand aunt) Miss ADELAIDE COOKE!!!
Lounge, (a literacy fop, betrothed to Flourish and intriguing with Bridget) Miss ADELAIDE COOKE!!!!
Mademoiselle Josephine, (an actress from Paris)... .. .... Miss ADELAIDE COOKE!!!!!

PATTON, PRINTER, CHURCH ST. BIRMINGHAM.

One of the long forgotten theatres in Birmingham.
It was only open a few years. Period 1835 to 1838.

DAY'S CONCERT HALL,
SMALLBROOK STREET.

Special Engagements for the Christmas Holidays.

GRAND NEW BALLET,
entitled, THE

QUEEN BEE.
Supported by Well-known Artistes.

December 1877

NEW SCENERY NEW COSTUMES!

NEW SONGS!!!

NEW THEATRE ROYAL, rear of 83 Moor Street.
    Opened in 1861.   Lessee and Manager John C. Chute.   On Sep. 4 of this year it presented the dramatic romance, "The Midnight Phantom" or "The Angel of Death".   (see poster for full details).   On Sep. 16 another dramatic romance was presented, "Willow Copse" and the drama of "The Wreck Ashore".   In the Christmas period each year a pantomime was produced, in January 1862 "Cinderella" or, "The Prince, the Fairy, and the Little Glass Slipper", was presented.   Prices of admission, Boxes 2s, Pit 1s, Gallery 6d.   The programmes commenced nightly at half past seven.   Children in arms NOT admitted.   Smoking in the theatre strictly prohibited.   Police in attendance to preserve order.   In 1863 the proprietor was Mr. Walton.   The theatre closed this year when the building and adjacent buildings were demolished to make way for the construction of Dale End.

69

The New ADELPHI THEATRE, rear of 66 Moor Street, opened c.1863, the sole Lessee and Manager was Mr. H.P. Grattan. Brilliant Chandeliers were erected to grace the interior of the building. It was forced to close in 1864 when the building and adjacent ones had to be demolished to make way for the construction of Albert Street.

Moor Street was one of the main city centre streets at this time proceeding from the Bull Ring to Stafford Street. All that is left of it now is the entrance to Moor Street Station. It is now known as The Queensway and Moor Street, Queensway.

A mystery theatre (or circus). No positive records of this in Birmingham Directories and no year shown on this programme. It was in the mid 19th century, of that I am certain but, was it a marquee on open ground, rented for the season. According to the Encyclopaedic Dictionary an amphitheatre is an oval or circular building with seats rising in tiers round an open arena.

71

MUSEUM CONCERT HALL,
BULL RING.

General Manager ....Mr. R. G. GOLDSMITH.

PATRICK FEENEY, the Great "Shaughraun;"
HARMAN and ELSTON, Royal Negroists;
BAILEY'S PUNCH AND JUDY, DURDEN and
STORM, ETTY GRAY, FLORENCE KIRBY,
FRED. ETMFRD, and Star Concert Company.
HARRY WINGETT at Christmas.
The Old Prices: Floor 6d., half returned; Balcony
6d.; Reserved Seats 1s.   109

December 1877

The LONDON MUSEUM and CONCERT HALL, 143 Digbeth, opened on the 24th December 1863. Proprietor George Biber. In 1890 it changed its name to Canterbury Tavern and Music Hall, proprietor Alex. MacGregor. In 1894 it was taken over by Alfred Hardy and he changed the name to Pavilion Tavern and Music Hall. In 1896 Harry Ashmore took over and changed it to its original name. In the same year William Coutts took over and called it, Coutts' Theatre. This continued for 2 years. He was a great man and on Sundays held Lantern Services in connection with Mr. Pentland's Street Robins Movement. Numerous outings were arranged for poor children to be taken on trips to the country. It closed in 1900. In 1912 it opened as The Bull Ring Cinema. This building was originally in Digbeth on the corner of Park Street but in 1897 The Royal George Public House was built in front of it, the address then changed to No.2 Park Street. The building is still there today.

The UNICORN INN and CONCERT HALL, 46 Digbeth, Birmingham. Opened c. 1885 presenting a variety of programmes for patrons. It was under the management of R.G. Goldsmith who was for several years the manager of the London Museum and Concert Hall.

10

THE MODERN BULL RING

The MODERN BULL RING area, this was officially opened by
The Prince of Wales on the 29th May 1964.

THE ROTUNDA
An office building
which towers behind the
new open market area.

The MARKET HALL, this opened on the 14th November 1963, it has
155 General Traders and 42 Fish and Poultry sections.

MANZONI GARDENS, on the site of the old Market Hall.

The ROW MARKET, situated in Edgbaston Street next to the Rag Market, this opened in June 1977. It has 90 stalls which specialise in modern clothing for the younger set. It covers the old Jamaica Row area. It is open on Tuesdays, Fridays and Saturdays.

The FLEA MARKET, adjacent to the Row Market, opened in 1979, it has proved to be a very popular venue, it has 140 stalls which offer an assortment of wares, second-hand equipment, tools, household goods, toys, books, hot dog stall and a meat auction stall. It is on the site of the Old St. Martin's Hotel, and on the corner of Moat Lane.

FLEA MARKET walkway, Birmingham Wholesale Market
is in the background.

This is the present RAG MARKET, held in St. Martin's Market in Edgbaston Street. It opened in August 1957. It has a staggering 550 stalls under one roof. The variety of goods offered is innumerable, ranging from second hand goods, crockery, bed linen, perfume and jewellery. The atmosphere within the market is exciting. It is open at 10.00 am on Tuesday, Friday and Saturday.

11

THE BULL RING TOMORROW

Since the completion of this book, a scheme has now been dev-
eloped, to completely refurbish the area and give it a new look, at a cost
of £320 million . The Rotunda Office block is to be demolished. The
markets in Edgbaston Street will be re-built in a tree lined street. This
scheme of construction work will ensure no interruption in the business
of traditional markets, these will be preserved and improved. A £1 million
superbowl, at 90ft across, has been designed to replace the present symbol
of the area. It will have well-lit and patrolled pedestrian arcades providing
24 hour access through the 26 acre site. It will have a newly paved and
landscaped square, this will be the base for open markets and provide
even more public space area (see map for details) Smallbrook Queensway
will be lowered, with the shopping development sitting on top of it, to
allow a ground level pedestrian access from New Street and High Street
down a gently sloping concourse leading to St. Martin's Church. These
alterations will be built in phases, and hopefully be completed by 1996.

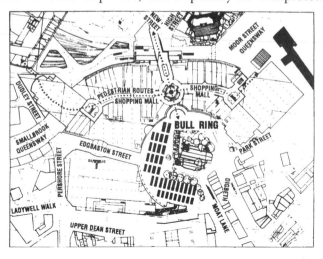